D1124350

Mighty Bots

ANIMAL ROBOTS

THOMAS KINGSLEY TROUPE

WORLD BOOK

This World Book edition of *Animal Robots*
is published by agreement between
Black Rabbit Books and World Book, Inc.

2140 Howard Dr. West,
North Mankato, MN 56003 U.S.A.
World Book, Inc.,
180 North LaSalle St., Suite 900,
Chicago, IL 60601 U.S.A.

Jennifer Besel, editor; Grant Gould, interior designer; Michael Sellner, cover designer; Omay Ayres, photo researcher

Library of Congress Control Number: 2016049961

ISBN: 978-0-7166-9329-1

Printed in the United States at CG Book Printers,
North Mankato, Minnesota, 56003. 3/17

Image Credits

Alamy: Alfo Co. Ltd., 24 (bottom); PhotoStock-Israel, 28; Stuart Abraham, 29; AP Images: FEREX, 16–17; Boston Dynamics: WildCat Robot images courtesy of Boston Dynamics, 6; Getty Images: ADRIAN DENNIS, 24 (top); MARK RALSTON, 4–5, 9 (WildCat); Svetlana Foote, 8 (cheetah); Science & Society Picture Library, 25; http://kamigamirobots.com/: Dash Robotics, 26; http://orb.olin.edu/: Orlin Robotics and Bioinspiration Lab, 14 (DynaRoACH); http://www.darpa.mil/: DEFENSE ADVANCED RESEARCH PROJECTS AGENCY, 11; iStock: higyou, 22–23, 31; Newscom: Sorokin Donat/ZUMA Press, 14 (Death's Head); phys.org: Daniel Goldman, 15; Shutterstock: AKKHARAT JARUSILAWONG, 8–9 (background); DM7, 3; Elena11, 12; Gwoeii, 1, Back Cover; Ocalacia, Cover; Sm.Shakhov, 32; think4photop, 27; www.festo.com/bionics: Festo AG & Co. KG, 17, 18, 21 (both); FRANCK ROBICHON/EPA, 19

CONTENTS

CHAPTER 1

A Wild ROBOT

A small engine hums and whines. A four-legged creature races along the road. It goes faster with each step. It moves like a cheetah. But it doesn't look like one. It's WildCat!

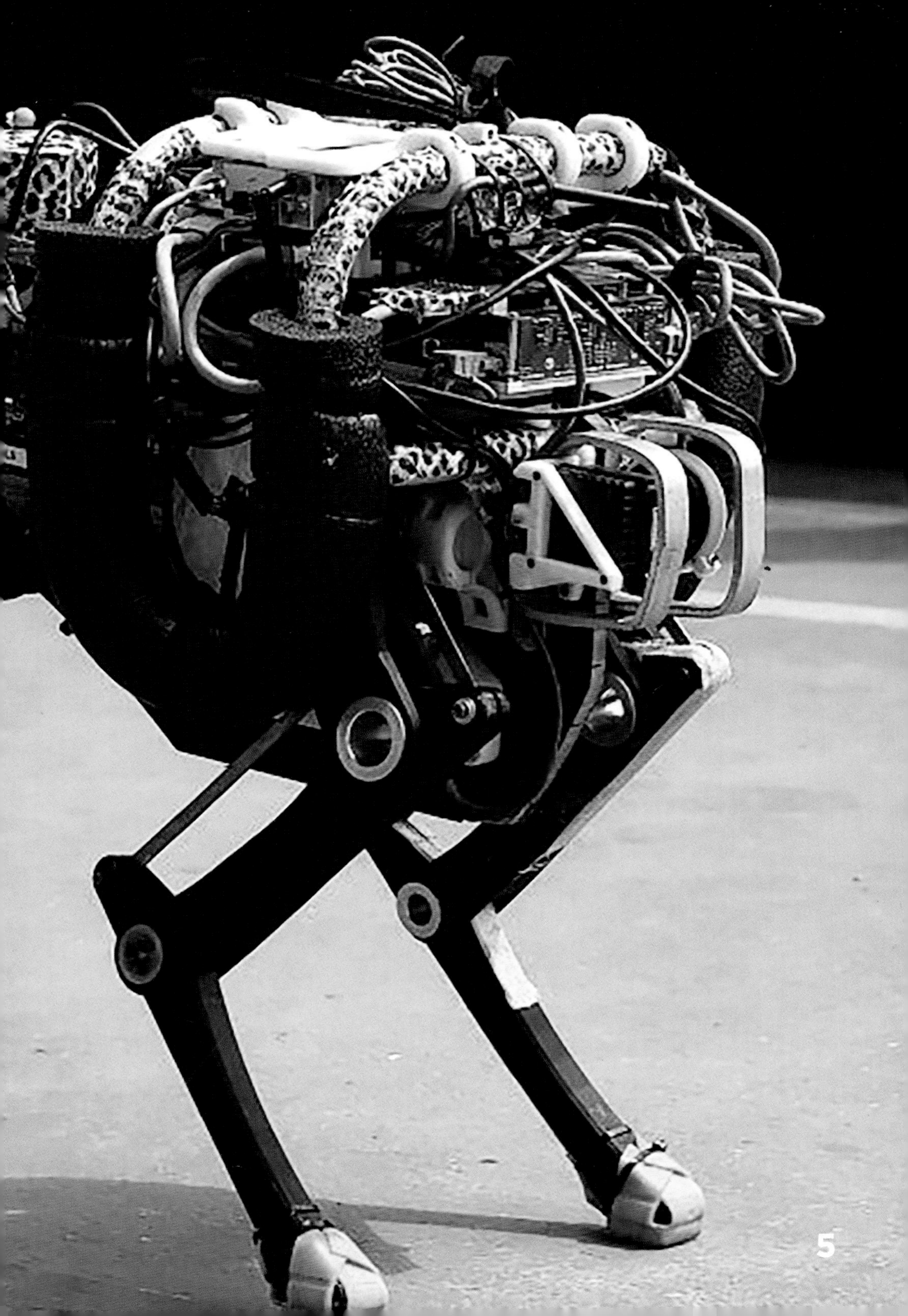

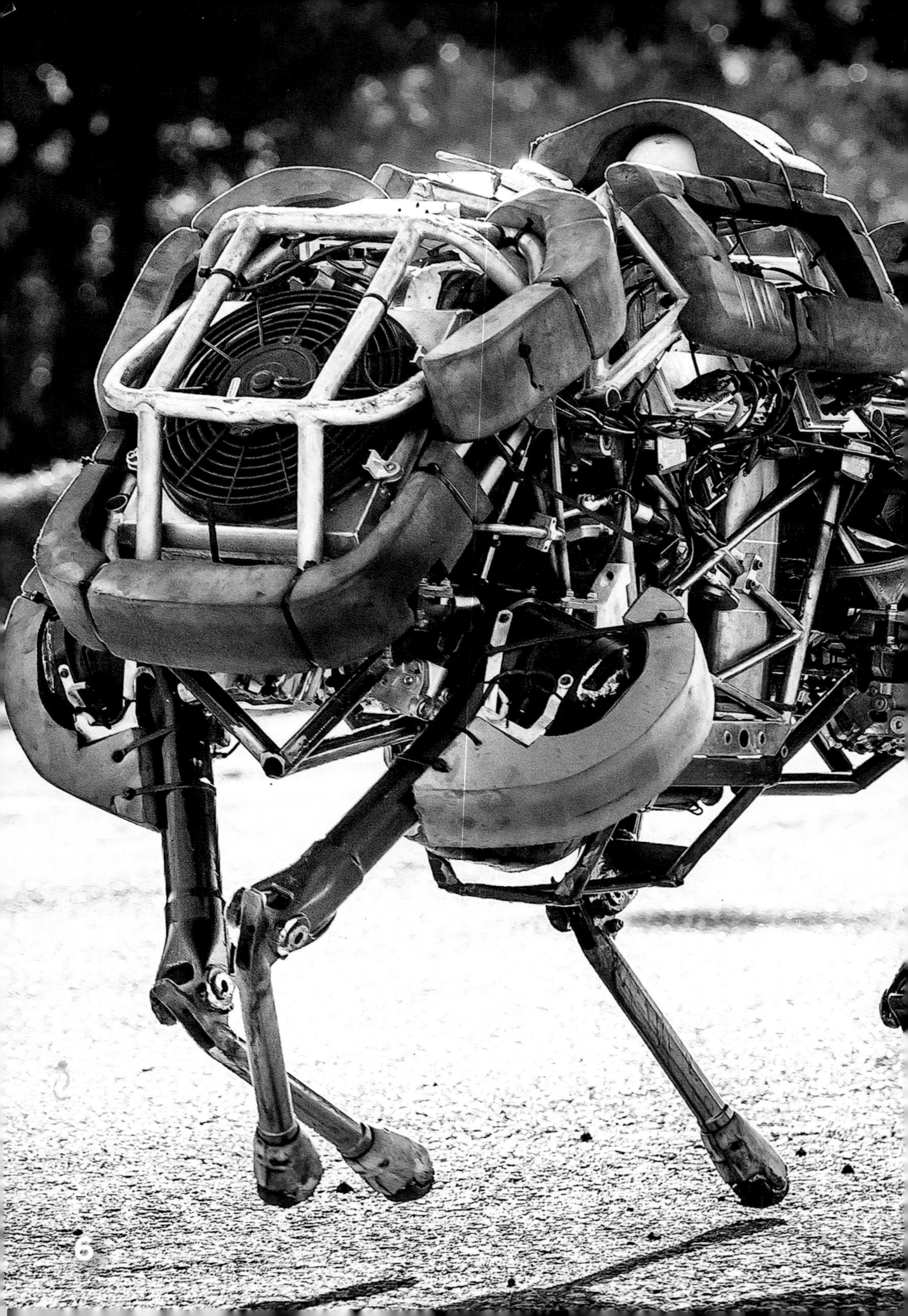

Speed Machine

The WildCat robot runs up to 16 miles (26 kilometers) per hour. This amazing robot isn't a pet. It's a speed machine. It might one day chase enemies during war.

An early version of WildCat is called Cheetah. Cheetah can run 29 miles (47 km) per hour on a treadmill.

Cheetah

TOP SPEED
70 MILES
(113 KM) PER HOUR

HEIGHT
about 2.5 feet
(1 meter)

ENERGY SOURCES
meat and water

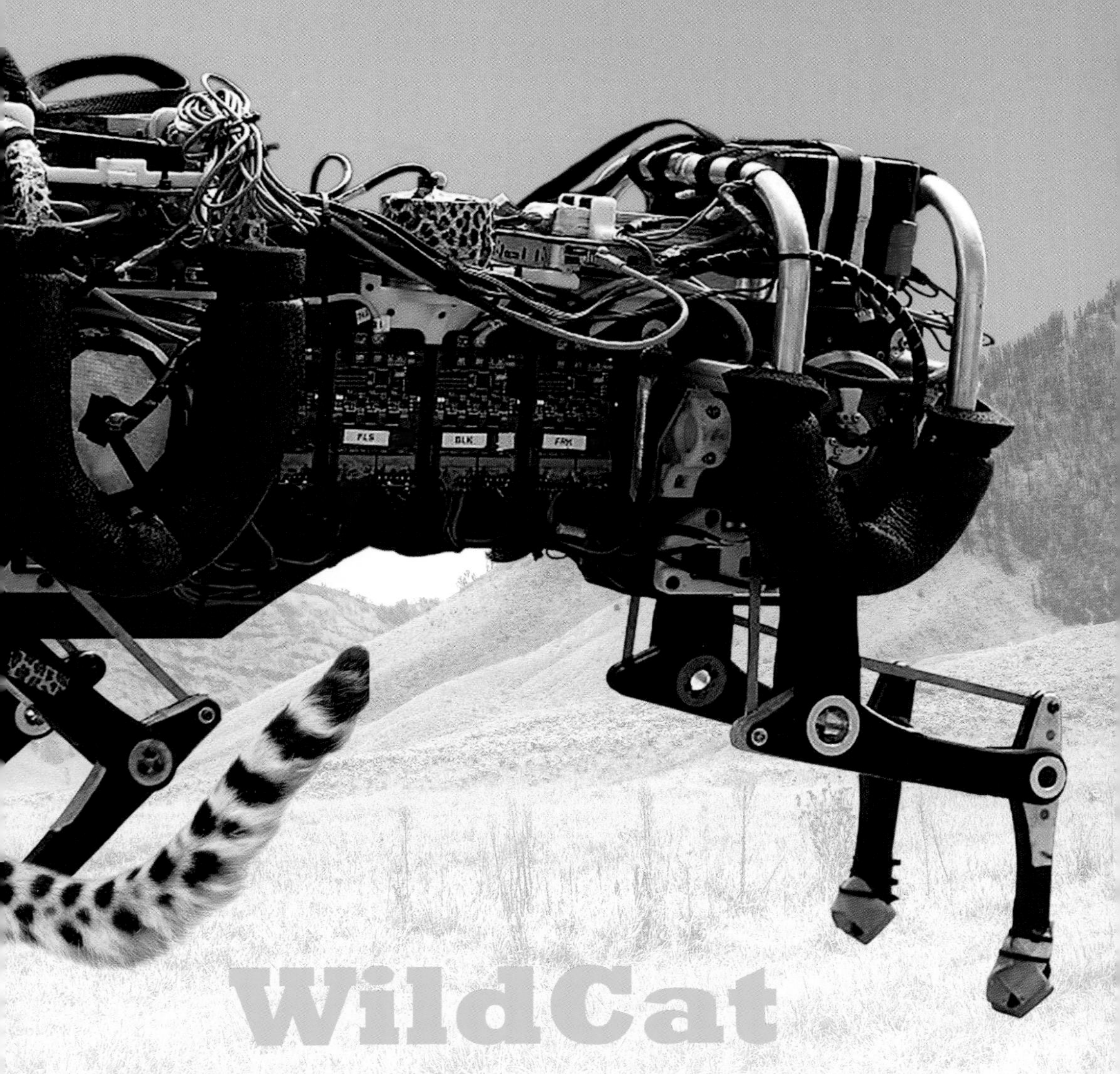

WildCat

TOP SPEED
16 MILES
(26 KM) PER HOUR

HEIGHT
about 2.5 feet
(1 m)

ENERGY SOURCE
gasoline

CHAPTER 2

Building ROBOT Animals

Scientists have built animal robots for years. Right now, they are trying to make more **flexible** robots. Someday, they want robots to learn on their own.

One of the first animal robots was a duck. It was built around 1738. It moved and quacked. It could also eat and poop.

Learning From Real Life

Scientists study how real animals act. Then they design robots that use those **behaviors**. For example, real animals wiggle and squirm if they get stuck. Scientists make robots do the same thing.

ROBO-ROACHES!

Robot "bugs" scurry around labs.

DynaRoACH

LENGTH
3.94 inches
(10 centimeters)

WEIGHT
0.06 pound
(25 grams)

can move across sand

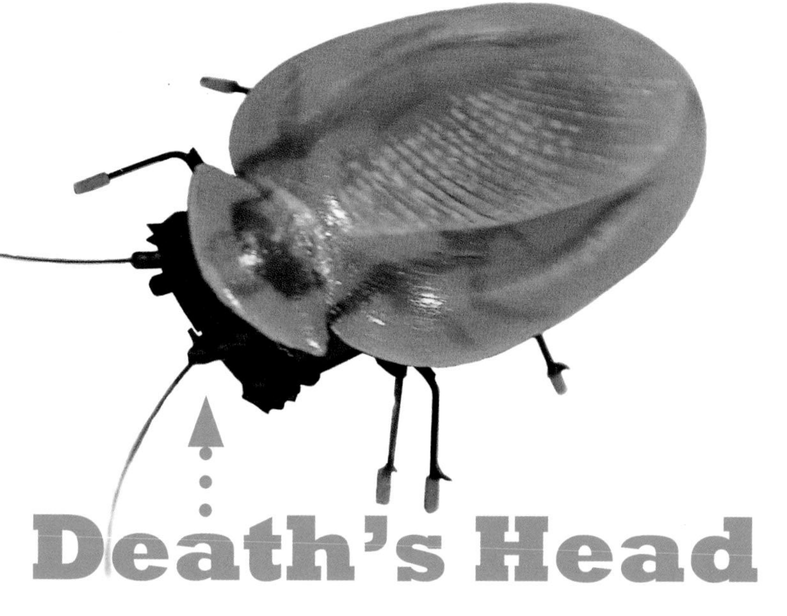

Death's Head

LENGTH
3.93 inches
(10 cm)

WEIGHT
top secret

looks like a real cockroach and might be good for spy missions

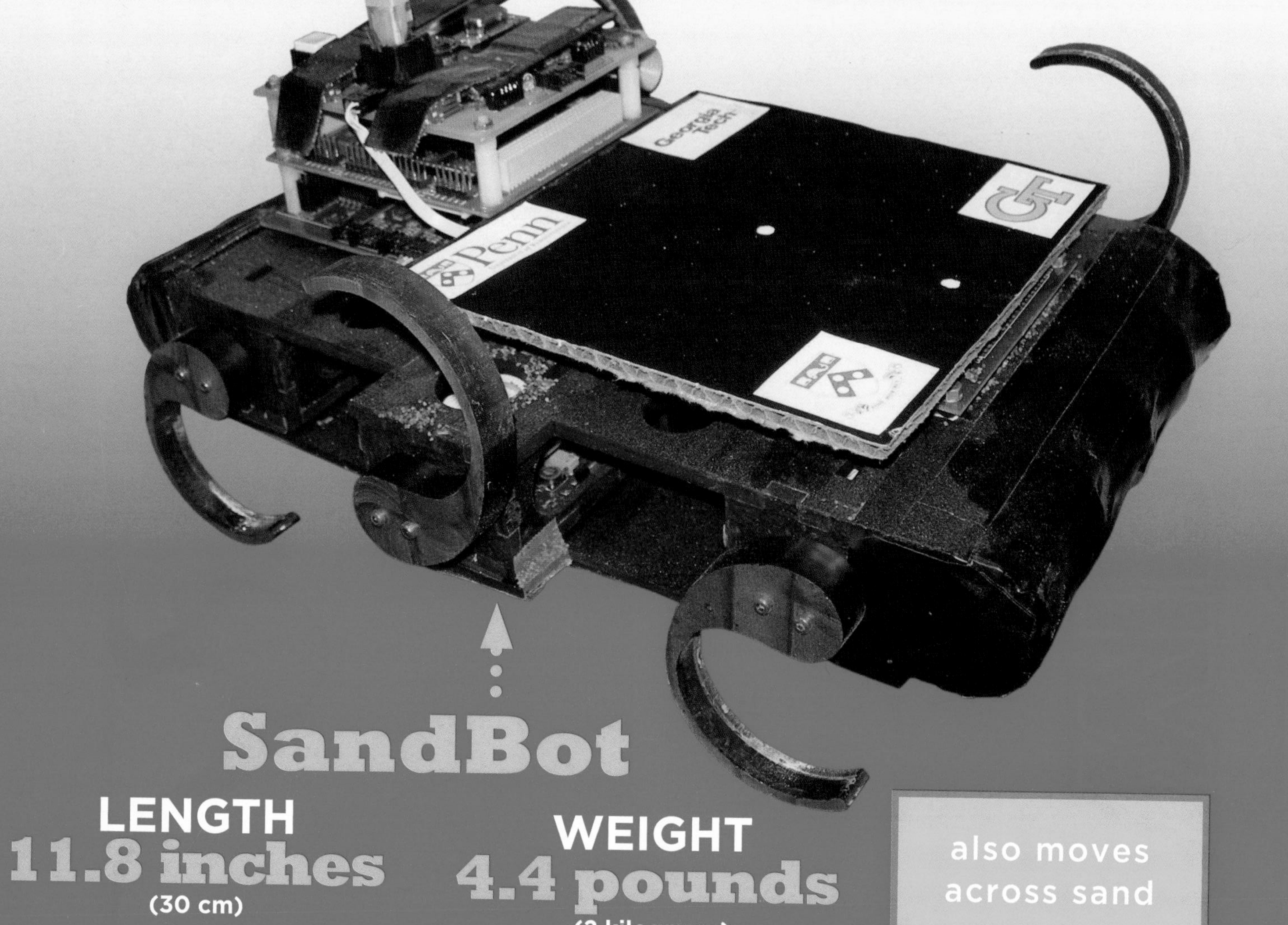

SandBot

LENGTH
11.8 inches
(30 cm)

WEIGHT
4.4 pounds
(2 kilograms)

also moves across sand

CHAPTER 3

WIRED Wildlife

Some animal robots do more than walk. Some fly, slither, or swim. **Bionic**Kangaroo can go more than 2 feet (1 m) with one hop.

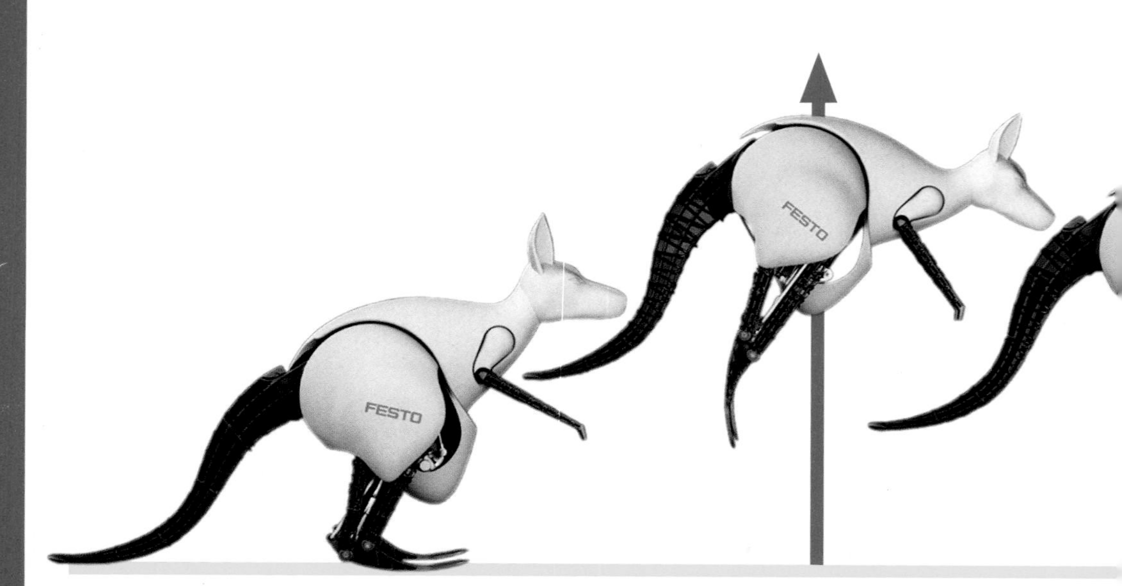

How Far BionicKangaroo Hops

horizontal hop
31 inches (79 cm)

FESTO

Robotic Sea Life

In Japan, designers built a snakelike robot. ACM-R5H wiggles on land. It also swims in water.

Underwater robots are built in Germany too. Aqua_ray acts like a manta ray. AquaJelly is like a jellyfish.

Flying Robots

It's not a bird. It's not a plane. It's a robot! SmartBird looks like a **gull**. It even flaps its wings to fly.

The BionicOpter looks like a dragonfly. It can fly and turn like the real animal. A person tells it where to fly with a remote control.

SmartBird can take off and land on its own.

FESTO

Who's Building Animal Bots?

Immanuel Kant Baltic Federal University in Russia
Death's Head

HiBot in Japan
ACM-R5H

ETH Zurich in Switzerland
Naro (a fish robot)

Robo-Fish

They swim like regular fish.

Sensors look for chemicals in the water.

They use batteries for power.

CHAPTER 4

HELPING Humans

Some animal robots help humans. A fish robot swims in oceans and lakes. It finds **pollution**. When a robo-fish **senses** pollution, it swims to it. People then know where to clean up the mess.

Robots to the Rescue

Robot cockroaches can be helpful. The DASH roach is quick and good at climbing. It can squeeze into tight spaces. One day, it might help find people after earthquakes.

A Robotic Zoo

Animal robots are fun and amazing. They can also be useful. Maybe one day, robot animals will fight in wars. Others will help during disasters. In time, there could be enough robot animals to fill a zoo. But please, don't feed the robots!

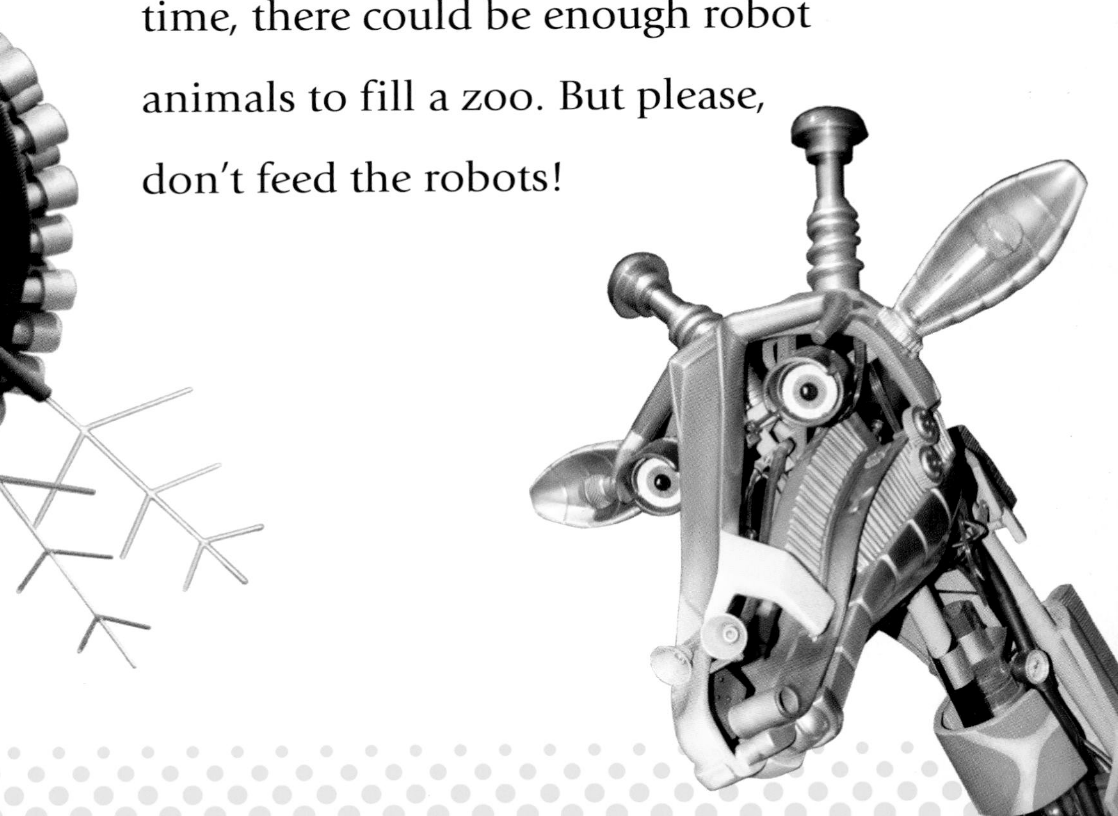

GLOSSARY

behavior (be-HAY-vyur)—the way a person or animal acts

bionic (bi-AH-nik)—having body parts made strong or more capable by electronic devices

chemical (KE-muh-kuhl)—a substance that can cause a change in another substance

flexible (FLEK-suh-bul)—able to change or do different things

gull (GUHL)—a long-winged bird that lives near water

pollution (puh-LOO-shun)—substances that make land, water, or air dirty and not safe to use

sense (SENS)—to detect the presence of something

sensor (SEN-sor)—a device that finds heat, light, sound, motion, or other things

LEARN MORE

BOOKS

Becker, Helaine. *Zoobots: Wild Robots Inspired by Real Animals.* Tonawanda, NY: Kids Can Press, 2014.

Faust, Daniel R. *Underwater Robots.* Robots and Robotics. New York: PowerKids Press, 2016.

Swanson, Jennifer. *National Geographic Kids. Everything Robotics: All the Robotic Photos, Facts, and Fun!* Everything Series. Washington, D.C.: National Geographic, 2016.

WEBSITES

Robotics
kidsahead.com/subjects/1-robotics

Robotics: Facts
idahoptv.org/sciencetrek/topics/robots/facts.cfm

Robots for Kids
www.sciencekids.co.nz/robots.html

INDEX